Microsoft

PowerPoint

2010

Ron Greener

Computer Services

Table of Contents

Introduction

This book has been prepared at the request of students taking MS PowerPoint within a community education setting. It will serve anyone whose goal is to gain PowerPoint skills for the workplace, college, or just general everyday use. The author has 35 years of teaching experience at the community college level. Overlapping that to some extent are 35 years of business world experience installing and maintaining mainframe computers. The book was designed to be an exact match to the delivery of the classroom material so that repetition at a later time is 100% possible. Feedback from this concept of training has been very positive.

Notice: All Rights Reserved.

Copying the material within this book is not permitted without the expressed permission of the author, Ron Greener, greener@lcc.edu, 810-227-3839

Computer Services

Microsoft PowerPoint 2010

WHAT IS POWERPOINT?

PowerPoint

1. Microsoft PowerPoint 2010 is presentation software with which you create electronic slide presentations. It is an ideal tool for teachers, lawyers, meetings, parties, convention booths, and even creating web pages that can then be posted on the WWW. PowerPoint presentations consist of a number of individual pages or "slides". The slide analogy is a reference to the former slide projector in which 35mm slides from a camera were inserted into a projector and presented in a magnified format. However, with PowerPoint, added functionally such as animation, transition, sound, color, and video can be added to create interest and retention. Typically the slides are navigated through by the presenter but it can also be setup to run unattended with preset timing. This works well for convention booths and storefronts.

PowerPoint provides three types of movements:

1. Entrance, emphasis, and exit of elements on a slide itself are controlled by what PowerPoint calls Custom Animations

2. Transitions, on the other hand, are movements between slides. These can be animated in a variety of ways.

3. Custom animation can be used to create small story boards by animating pictures to enter, exit or move.

Computer Services

Microsoft PowerPoint 2010

THE POWERPOINT WINDOW

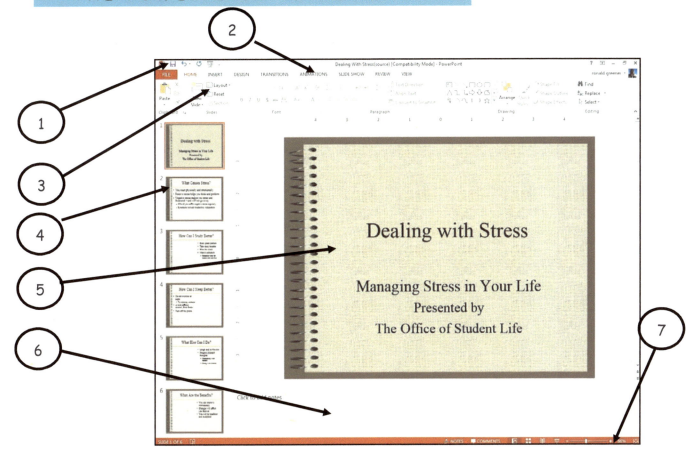

1. Quick Access Tool bar

2. Ribbon Tabs or Top Level Tabs

3. Ribbon

4. Navigation pane

5. Slide pane

6. Speaker Notes pane

7. Zoom

8. NOTE: The Quick Access Toolbar is meant to be a convenience to the user and thus provide efficiency. Commands can be easily added to it by right-clicking the command and clicking "Add to Quick Access Toolbar".

Computer Services

Microsoft PowerPoint 2010

SPEAKER NOTES PANE

1. This is an area shown at the bottom of each slide for making notes reminding you about important points in the active slide. They can be independently printed and then referred to during the presentation. The audience does not see them in the presentation.

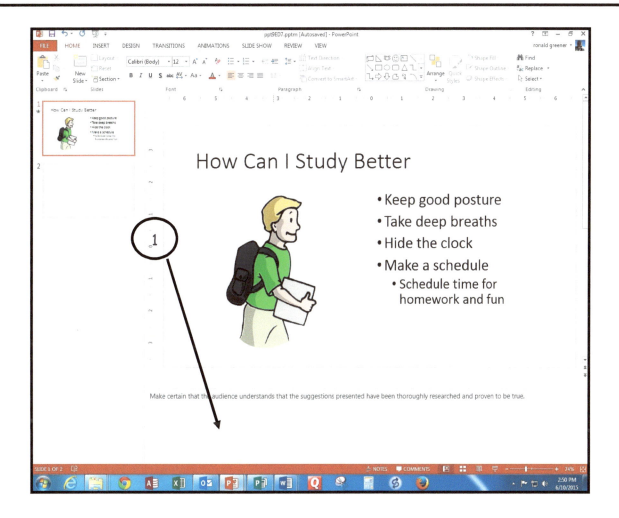

Computer Services

1. **Design**: the background artwork

2. **Layout**: the arrangement of the placeholders

3. **Placeholders**: Boxes wherein text is entered

4. **Transition**: The motion that the slide goes through in moving from one to the next

5. **Animation**: The motion that the content within the slide goes through

6. **Graphics**: Pictures and video within a slide

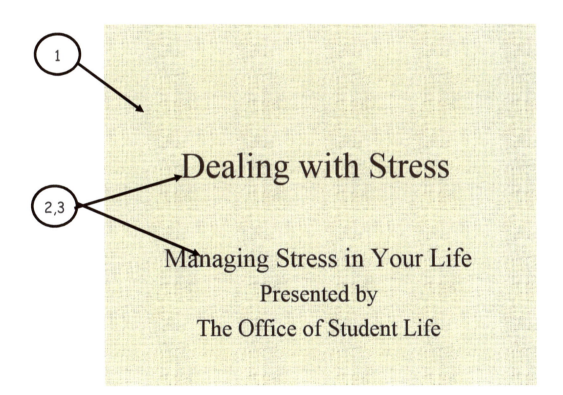

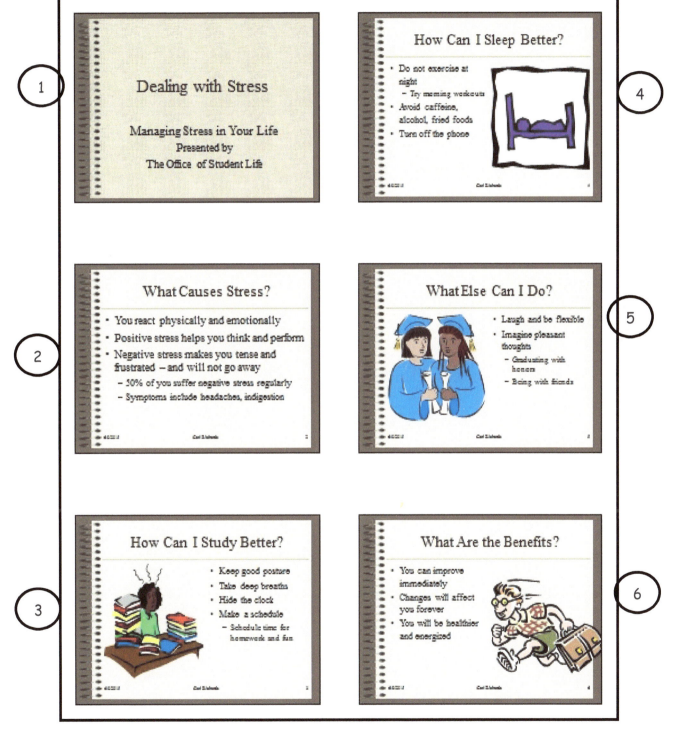

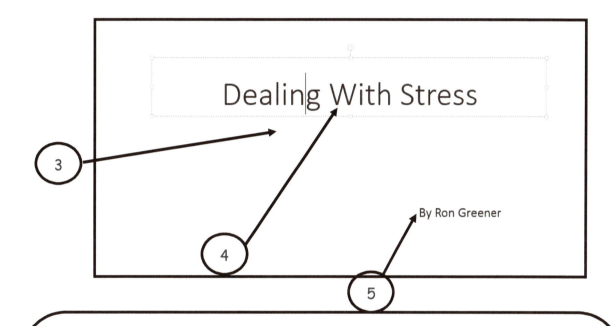

1. Open PowerPoint
2. Click the Blank template
3. A blank Title slide layout is generated
4. In the Title placeholder, enter "Dealing With Stress"
5. In the subtitle , enter By YOUR NAME or any PREFERRED CONTENT
6. **Note** that the place holders can be moved and resized
7. **Notice** that formatting from the Home tab ribbon can be applied to the text.

Computer Services

ADDING A SECOND SLIDE

ADDING A SECOND SLIDE

1. From the Home Tab, click New Slide

2. Click the Title and Content layout

3. Title Placeholder

4. Bulleted Text Placeholder

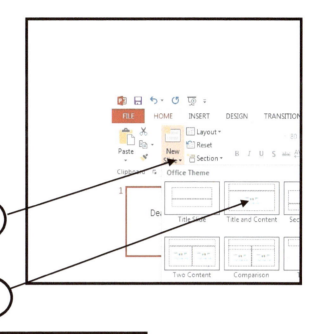

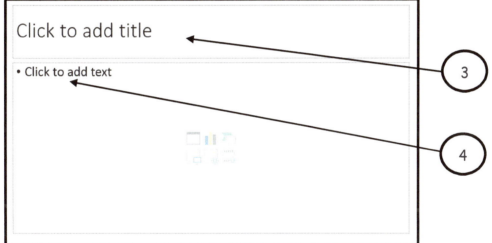

Computer Services

ENTERING CONTENT INTO THE PLACEHOLDERS

1. Click into the Title Placeholder and add text (capitalize each word)

2. Insert the bulleted text (first word capitalized)

3. Use the tab key to move the bullet to the second level, ie indented.

4. Use shift-tab to return the bullet back to the first level .

What Causes Stress? ①

 ②

- You react physically and emotionally

- Positive stress helps you think and perform

- Negative stress makes you tense and frustrated — and will not go away
  ③
  - 50% of you suffer negative stress regularly

  - Symptoms include headaches, indigestion

Computer Services

ADDING A SPLIT CONTENT SLIDE

1. Insert a New Slide,

2. Select Two Content layout

3. Click link to pictures

4. Click a picture which inserts it into the slide.. Note that it is floating and can be dragged around and resized.

5. Enter text into the Title and Bulleted List placeholders.

6. Use the tab key to indent bullets and shift-tab to return to first level indent

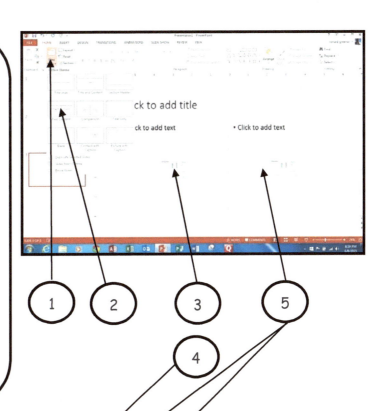

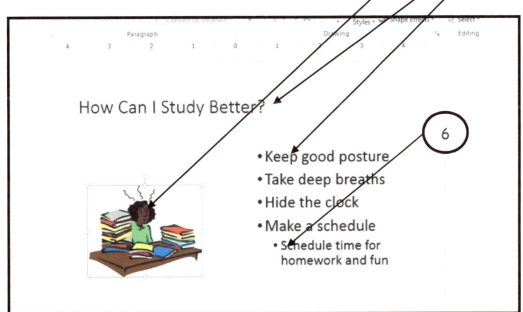

Computer Services

ADDING ADDITIONAL SLIDES

Repeat the previously stated procedures for the remaining slides

How Can I Sleep Better?

- Do not exercise at night
  - Try morning workouts
- Avoid caffeine, alcohol, fried foods
- Turn off the phone

What Else Can I Do?

- Laugh and be flexible
- Imagine pleasant thoughts
  - Graduating with honors
  - Being with friends

What Are the Benefits?

- You can improve immediately
- Changes will affect you forever
- You will be healthier and energized

Computer Services

Microsoft PowerPoint 2010

APPLY A DESIGN WITH A PRESET THEME

1. Design refers to the color and artwork that appears in the background

2. Click on the Design tab

3. Select one of the preset Theme Designs.

4. Note that the design is applied to all slides and the appearance and layout have been changed so as to comply with the theme.

5. Remove a Theme design by selecting the Office Theme.

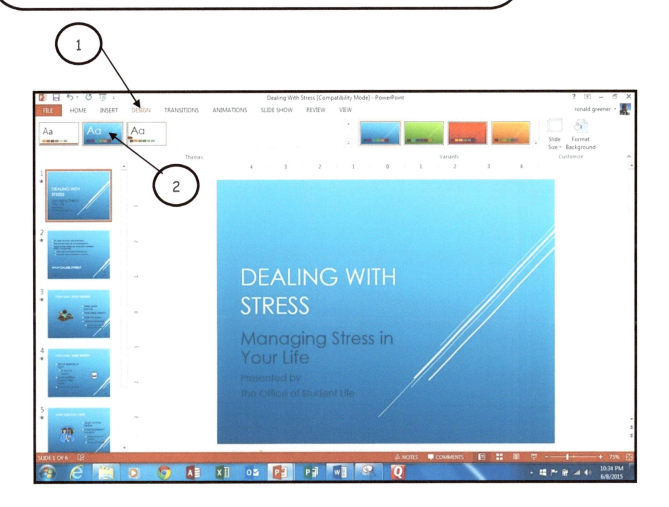

Computer Services

Microsoft PowerPoint 2010

1. Click on the Design tab

2. Click Format Background

3. Apply a Format Background feature such as color.

4. Note that it is applied to the selected slide only.

5. For an assortment of backgrounds, click one slide at a time and apply a Background Format.

6. Another choice following Step 3, is to click Apply to All.

7. Remove Background Formats with the Reset Background button.

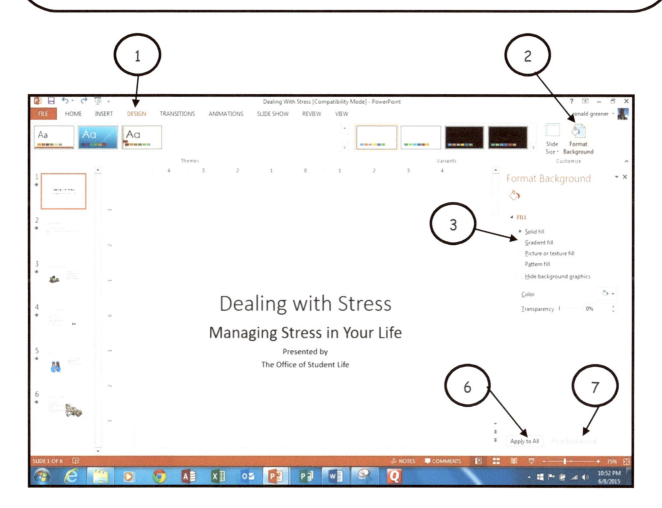

Computer Services

CHECKING ALL VIEWS

POWERPONT VIEWS

1. <u>**Normal View**</u> is the default view and is intended for editing the presentation

2. <u>**Slide Sorter View**</u> provides a thumbnail sketch of all slides and is useful for navigating through slides in a multi-slide presentation, re-arranging slides, and observing timings.

3. <u>**Slide Show View**</u> hides all editing content and shows the slide fully covering the display screen. It is used when presenting to the audience.

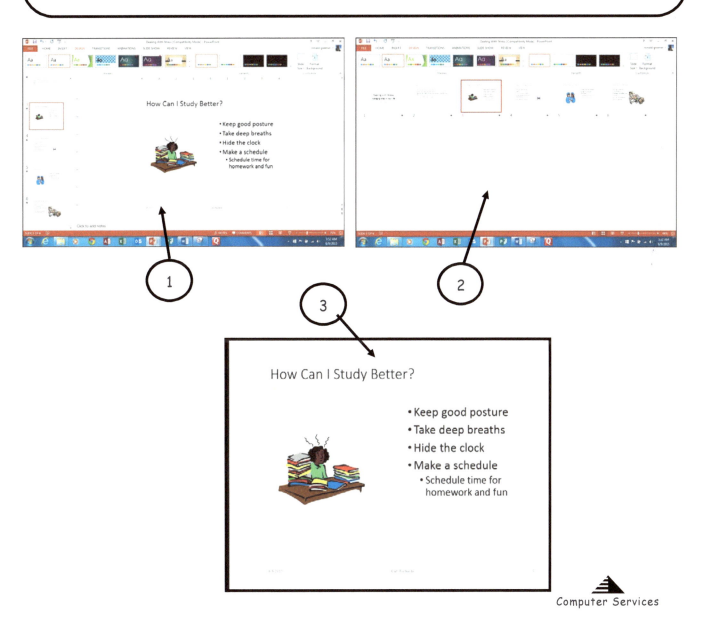

Computer Services

RUNNING THE SHOW (AUDIENCE MODE)

1. Click on the first slide to make it selected.

2. Click the Slide Show button in the lower right corner

3. Navigate through the slides using the left mouse or the left and right arrow keys

4. Notice the options that appear in the lower left corner as you hover the mouse over that area.

   - Forward/backward navigation
   - Pen for drawing and with color selection
   - Thumbnails for quickly jumping around in a highly populated presentation
   - Laser for directing attention

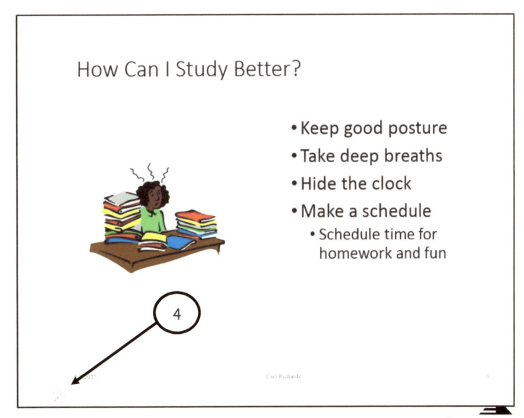

Computer Services

Microsoft PowerPoint 2010

APPLYING TRANSITION

TRANSITION: defined as the animation that a slide goes through when moving from one slide to the next.

1. Click the Transitions tab
2. Select one of the preset transitions
3. Notice that the transition is applied to only the selected slide
4. For consistent transition throughout, click Apply to All
5. Otherwise select individual slides and apply transition of choice.

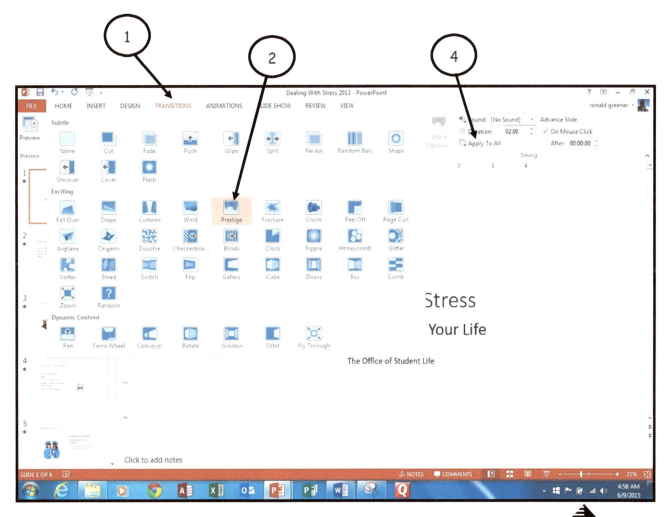

Computer Services

Microsoft PowerPoint 2010

APPLYING ANIMATION I

ANNIMATION: defined as the movement that the objects within a slide go through once the slide is in place.

1. Click the Animations tab
2. Select one of the objects such as the Title Placeholder.
3. Click the Add Animation button on the ribbon
4. Click one of the Entrance animations
5. Repeat the above for each of the other objects
6. While Entrance Animations are demonstrated here, additional animation can also be applied following the entrance.

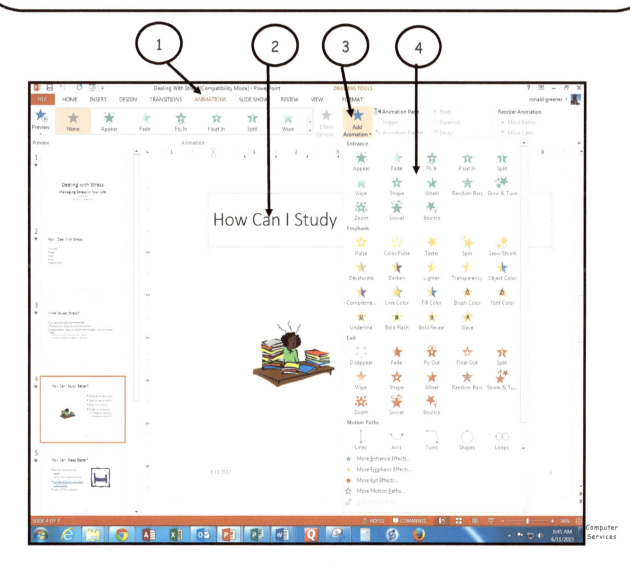

APPLYING ANIMATION II

When you have animated the objects in a slide, the sequence of the animation is displayed next to the object. In the case below, :

1. Title Placeholder first

2. The picture second

3. The bulleted text , third, fourth, fifth, and sixth

4. Notice that the Animation Pane displays the sequence as well

5. In the Animation Pane, you can drag the line item up or down to change the order.

6. Also in the Animation Pane, drop down each line item and select Effect Options and make changes to direction, timing, and whether to start on mouse click or "automatically after". And others.

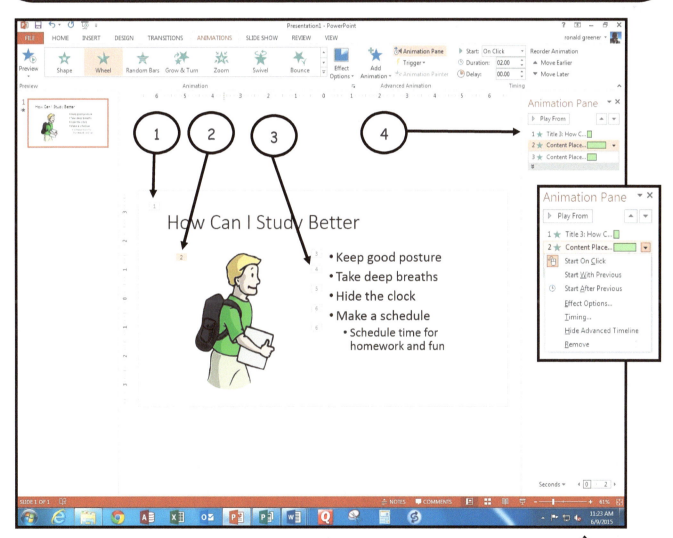

Computer Services

RUNNING AUTOMATIC WITH TIMINGS: in many cases it is appropriate to have the presentation running automatically, ie convention booth, customer waiting area, celebration parties, etc.

1. Click on the Transitions tab

2. In the Timing group, checkmark After and uncheck Mouseclick.

3. Upclick the timer to say 00:04.00 meaning 4 seconds so that transition occurs every 4 seconds for the selected slide.

4. Clicking Apply to All sets all slides to transition after 4 seconds.

5. Ignoring Step 4 above allows for a custom setting for each slide. This can be a better choice since slides vary in content therefore requiring more or less time for each one.

6. So as to loop continuously and therefore run non-stop, click the Slide Show tab (6a), then Setup Slide Show (6b), then checkmark Loop Until Escape (6c)

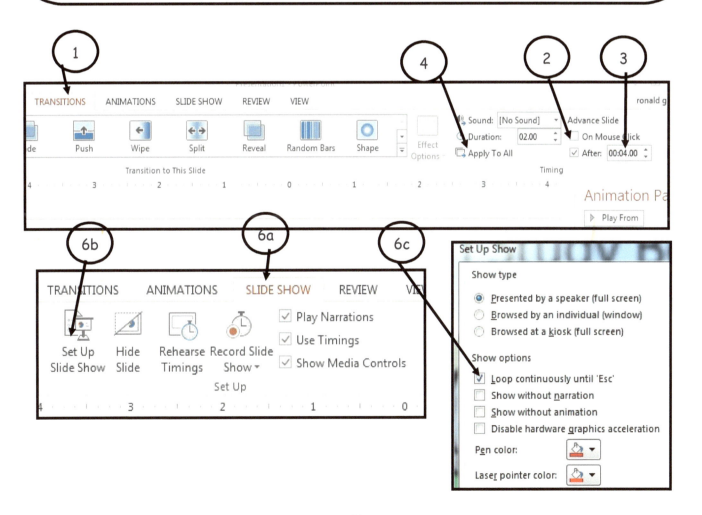

ADDING A SLIDE AND MOVING IT

1. Go to the Home tab

2. Click new slide

3. Select layout of choice

4. Populate the content desired

5. From the navigation pane, use the left mouse to drag the thumbnail up/down to where it is to be shown.

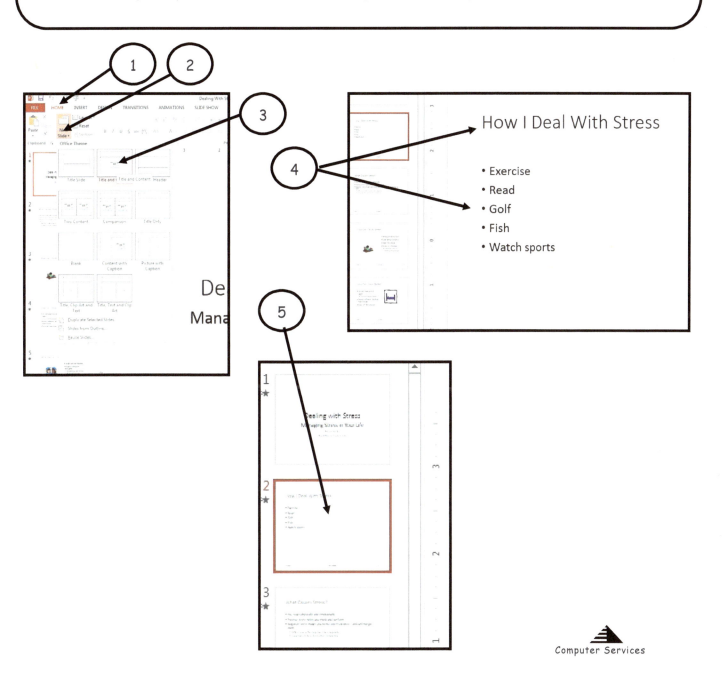

Computer Services

ADDING A HYPERLINK TO A SLIDE

<u>ADDING A HYPERLINK TO A SLIDE</u>

1. Open the webpage that is to be linked to

2. Highlight the address URL

3. Right-click the highlighted address and click Copy.

4. In the PowerPoint slide, select the text that is to be linked to the webpage.

5. Click the Insert tab

6. Click Hyperlink

7. Right-click and click Paste so as to put the address into the address box.

8. Go to Slide Show view. Click on the hyperlinked text to confirm that it opens the webpage

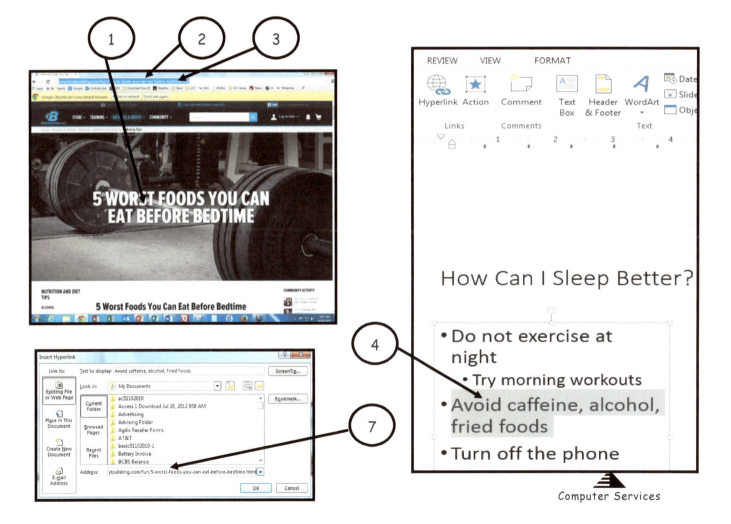

INSERTING A TEXT BOX

INSERTING A TEXT BOX

1. Click the Insert tab.

2. Click Text Box

3. Drag the down-pointing arrow so as to form a box at the intended location.

4. Type text as desired.

5. Adjust the size of the box using the sizing handles (shown only when selected)

6. Adjust the size and color of the text using the formatting features found within the Home tab.

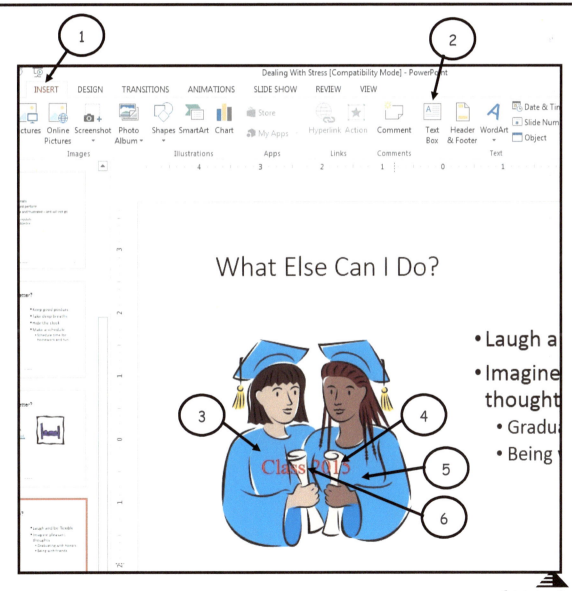

INSERTING AUTOSHAPES

INSERTING AN AUTOSHAPE

1. Click the Insert tab.

2. Click Shapes

3. Click the shape of choice

4. Use the crosshair on the mouse and drag at the desired location to form the shape.

5. Click into the center of the Autoshape so as to place the cursor there.

6. Type text as needed.

7. With the Autoshape selected, click the Home tab and use the formatting tools to set the fill color, font size and color.

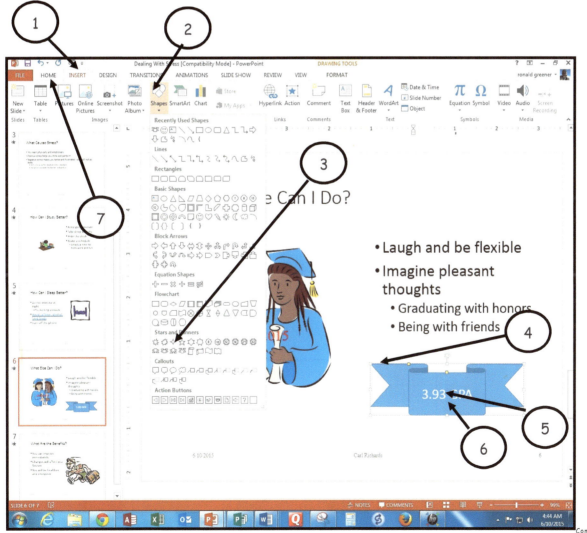

PRINTING SLIDES

PRINTING SLIDES

1. Click File

2. Select Print

3. Pull down on Full Page Slides

4. Select from:

   - Full Page

   - Notes

   - Handouts

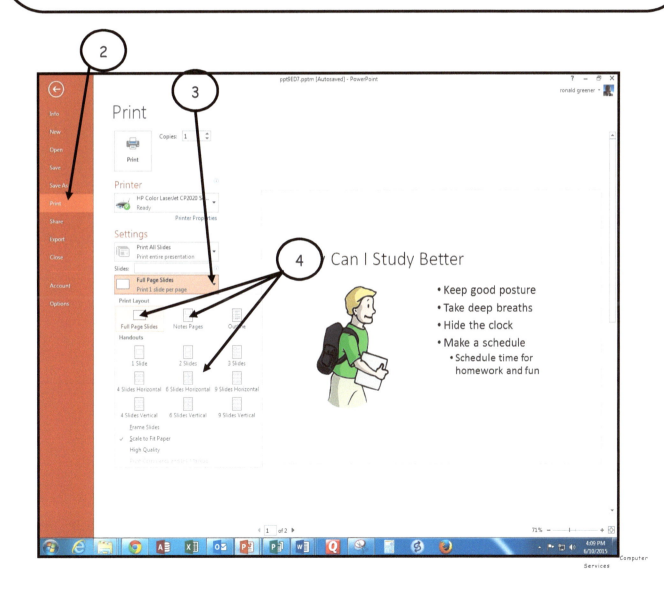

51

SAVING THE PRESENTATION

SAVING TO THE HARD DISK (PERMANENT SAVE)

1. The first time saving a PP file requires doing a SAVE AS command so as to provide a file name and a folder in which to save the file.

2. Click File on the left of the ribbon.

3. Click Save As

4. Enter a file name in the File Name box

5. Click the Documents Library.

6. Click New Folder and enter a name for the folder

7. Tap Enter twice so as to open the folder

8. Click Save which then saves the specified file into the specified folder in the Documents Library.

9. Since the document now has a name and location, all further saves require just a click of the SAVE command.

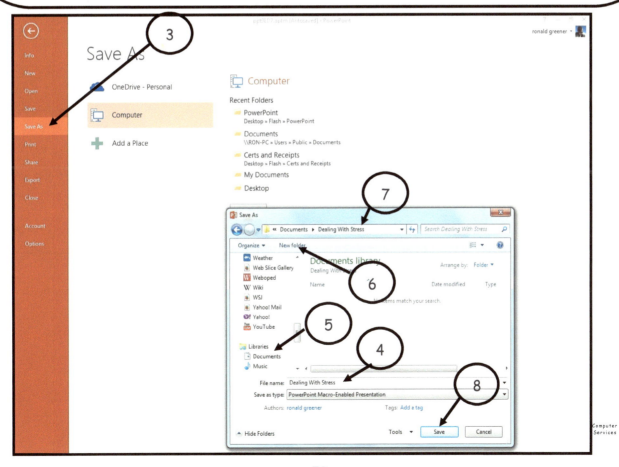

SAVING THE PRESENTATION IN SHOW MODE

SAVING IN SHOW MODE

1. Once the presentation is ready for presenting to an audience, it needs to be saved in Show Mode meaning that a special second file is saved (PPS: PowerPoint Show) This is the file used when giving the presentation. This file will bypass all of the editing areas and go straight to the show.

2. The steps are all the same as for the previous slide except for one thing: When Save As is clicked and the file name entered (Step 4), change the SAVE AS TYPE to PowerPoint Show.

3. Click Save.

4. Close the PP document.

5. Verify by opening the Documents Library and locate the new PPS file. Double-click it and it should open straight into Show Mode.

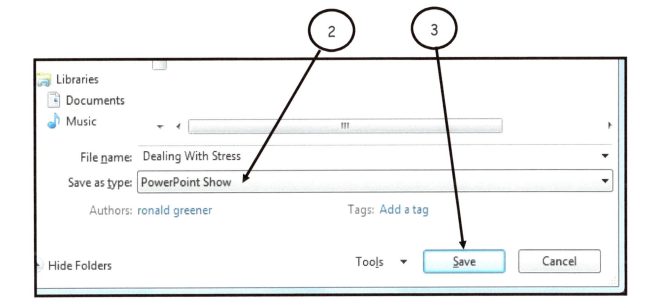

Computer Services

CREATING A PHOTO ALBUM

1. Photo Album in PowerPoint is a feature wherein all slides are pictures. Once loaded, transition is applied to all slides, plus music and timings so that the presentation runs on its own.

2. Open a New, Blank presentation.

3. Click Insert, Photo Album, and New Photo Album

4. Click the File/Disk button

5. Open the desired pictures folder in the Pictures Library

6. Select the desired pictures (use the CTRL key for scattered group, the SHIFT key for contiguous)

7. Click Insert

8. The selected pictures should then show as slides in the PP Navigation Pane on the left.

9. Continue steps 3-8 to add more pictures.

10. Refer to the previous procedures for adding **Transition** and **Timing** and **Loop Until ESC**

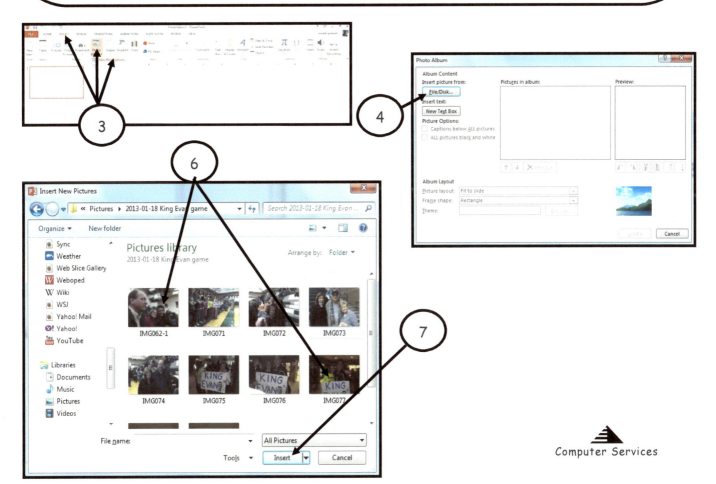

Computer Services

Microsoft PowerPoint 2010

ADDING MUSIC TO THE SLIDESHOW

ADDING MISIC

1. Click Insert tab

2. Click audio (speaker icon)

3. Browse to Song of choice and click Insert

4. Click on the speaker icon

5. Click on Audio Tools Playback

6. Click start automatically

7. Checkmark play across slides

8. Go into Show Mode and verify that the song plays through all slides.

9. Additional songs can be added to the slide where the previous song ends.

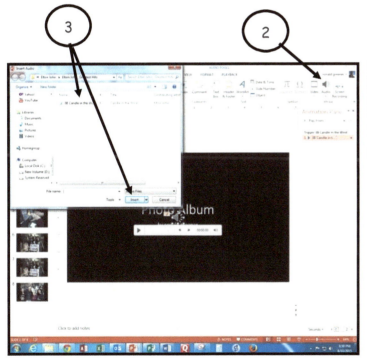

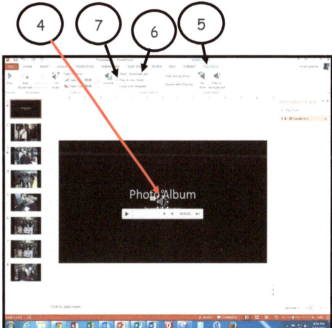

Computer Services

FLY ACROSS

1. Insert a blank slide.

2. Zoom the screen to 50% (red area)

3. Apply a design, say light red, full slide.

4. Insert a picture of a car.

5. Size it down .

6. Drag it to the left and outside of the left edge

7. Click on the car

8. Animation tab

9. Add animation

10. Lines

11. Drag the red dot attached to the second car to the point of destination

12. Play the slide. On a mouse click the car should travel across the screen

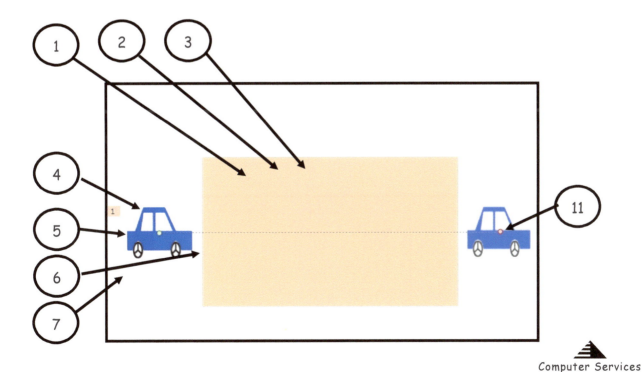

Computer Services

BLUE ANGELS FLY ACROSS

1. This is a step up from the previous page.

2. Go to google Images and download the picture "Blue Angels".

3. Then add four jet airplanes on the left

4. Add the animation as in the previous slide.

5. Enable the Animation Pane.

6. Cause all 4 planes to start at the same time

7. Make some fly fast and some slow

Computer Services

Microsoft PowerPoint 2010

LINKING TO PAGES, A BOOK CONCEPT

<u>LINKING TO PAGES</u>

This exercise demonstrates how to turn off the "transition to the next slide on mouse click". Instead, the navigation to slides is done by clicking on links in a table of contents (index). When the link is clicked, it opens a corresponding page of information. The page of information is then linked back to the table of contents. Our example is a list of titles of recipes on the first page that are setup as links to the recipe itself. In turn the recipe page is linked back to the table of contents. This concept is more of a book than a slide presentation.

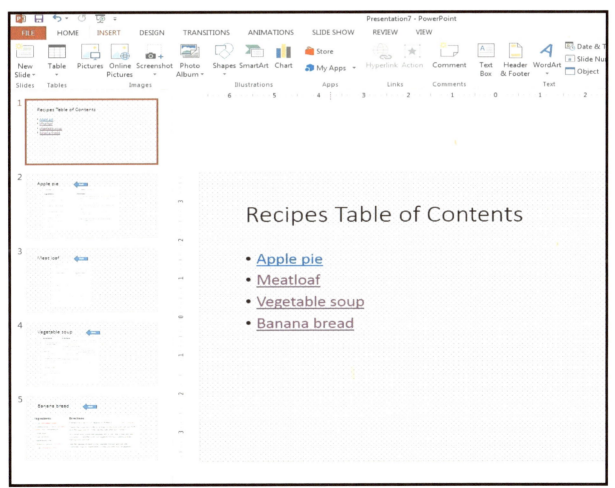

Computer Services

CREATING A RECIPE BOOK

1. Go to the Transitions tab and uncheck Advance Slide on Mouse Click.

2. Insert the first slide and set the layout to be that of "title and bulleted list"

3. Fill in the Title Placeholder

4. Fill in the bulleted list

5. Add information slides pertaining to each of the bulleted list items.

6. Link the text in each of the bullet lines to the corresponding pages

   - Click on the Insert tab

   - Action icon

   - Dot the "Hyperlink To"

   - Click on the drop-down and select Slide

   - Select the slide title that is to be linked to

   - Repeat for each of the Table of Contents items

7. In each of the information slides, insert a "back arrow" symbol

8. Right click on the symbol and click "Text". Then enter the word "Back"

9. Link the arrow symbol back to the Table of Contents slide.

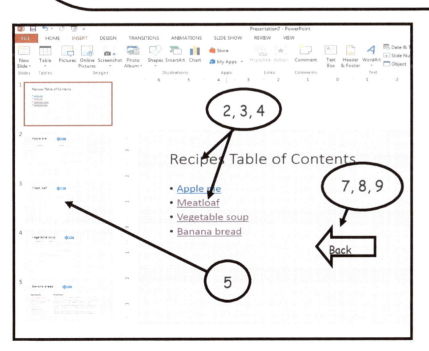

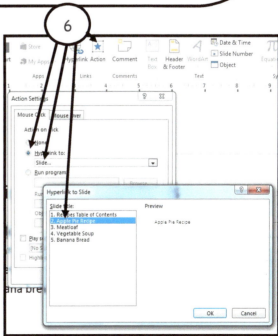